Communicate!

Memorable Lines

ice

Publishing Credits

Rachelle Cracchiolo, M.S.Ed., *Publisher*
Conni Medina, M.A.Ed., *Managing Editor*
Nika Fabienke, Ed.D., *Series Developer*
June Kikuchi, *Content Director*
Michelle Jovin, M.A., *Associate Editor*
Courtney Roberson, *Senior Graphic Designer*

TIME and the TIME logo are registered trademarks of TIME Inc. Used under license.

Image Credits: p.6 Andy Kazie/iStock; p.8 (bottom) Silver Screen Collection/Getty Images; p.9, p.17 Pictorial Press Ltd/Alamy; p.10, p.13, p.16, p.19, p.26, p.28, pp.34–35 AF archive/Alamy; p.12, pp.36–37, p.38 (insert) United Archives GmbH/Alamy; p.14 (center) Andrew Twort/Alamy; p.14 (bottom) Julie Clopper/Shutterstock; p.15 Featureflash Photo Agency/Shutterstock; p.20 WENN Ltd/Alamy; p.21 Illustration by Pilar Posada; p.24 4kclips/Shutterstock; p.25 Glasshouse Images/Newscom; p.27 ScreenProd/Photononstop/Alamy; p.29 Moviestore collection Ltd/Alamy; pp.30–31, p.32 (bottom) Photo 12/Alamy; pp.32–33 Entertainment Pictures/Alamy; p.34 (insert) Columbia Pictures/Album/Newscom; p.37 (insert) Erin Cadigan/Shutterstock; pp.38–39 RGR Collection/Alamy; p.40 CBS via Getty Images; p.41 NASA; all other images from iStock and/or Shutterstock.

Teacher Created Materials

5301 Oceanus Drive
Huntington Beach, CA 92649-1030
www.tcmpub.com

ISBN 978-1-4258-5014-2

© 2019 Teacher Created Materials, Inc.

Table of Contents

I Know That One!

There is a good chance that someone you know has quoted a favorite line from a movie, novel, play, song, television show, or other entertainment source sometime today. And you probably knew exactly where that line originated, because you have seen, heard, or read it. Maybe you were even able to quote the line that follows it!

We do this regularly—share memorable lines from our favorite forms of entertainment. There are lines that become inside jokes among friends, lines that become part of family **lore**, lines that touch our hearts, and lines that are just so notable you *have* to say them yourself! Some of the most memorable lines are hundreds of years old, so why is it that we still repeat them today?

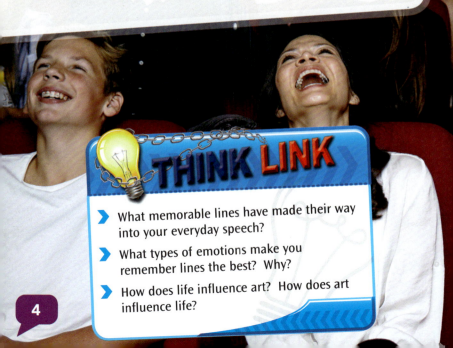

THINK LINK

> What memorable lines have made their way into your everyday speech?

> What types of emotions make you remember lines the best? Why?

> How does life influence art? How does art influence life?

All the Feels

Why do we remember some things and forget others? Emotion can play a part. Some studies suggest that the stronger the emotion a person feels during an experience, the more likely that person will remember the experience. Memory can also be "jogged." If a person "re-feels" an emotion, it can lead to a stronger recollection.

The Broadway musical *Hamilton* is one of the most successful (and quotable) shows of all time.

Earworms

An *earworm* is a piece of music that gets stuck in your head on a loop. Why this happens most likely has to do with having heard the music recently and repeatedly. It may also be tied to *involuntary memory,* which is when something seems to just pop into your head. This is usually because there has been some emotional trigger connecting a current experience to something in the past that the music was a part of.

There is probably a new line that you and your friends have been quoting recently. When someone says just the opening word or two, everyone swoops in to finish the line. Then, everyone follows it with a **plethora** of memorable lines, each one triggering the memory of another. Before long, a new line will probably catch your attention, sink into your memory, and become an addition to your quote **lexicon**. Will it come from a blockbuster movie, a bestselling book, a TV commercial, a smash Broadway show, or a song in the Billboard Top 100? Who knows? But no matter where it comes from, the line will instantly grab hold of you to become something you—and countless others—remember for a long, long time…

…ago…
…in a galaxy far, far away.

Advertising

People see and read advertisements a lot. They are everywhere—on billboards, on television, in magazines, on bus stops, on buildings…you name it! **Catchphrases** from popular ads often become part of a person's everyday speech. Depending on how old a person is, he or she likely remembers such lines as: "Where's the beef?"; "Silly rabbit!"; "They're grrreat!"; and many, many more.

Cool Catchphrases

Some lines are just so cool they *have* to be repeated—a lot. More often than not, they are the **signature** lines spoken by a character who is tough in the trendiest of ways. This character is larger than life—the kind of "awesome" many people fantasize about being.

I'll Be Back

When the main character says, "I'll be back," in 1984's *The Terminator*, many members of the audience get chills—and let out **ironic** laughs. The outrageous character had been denied entrance into a police station, so he comes "back" by driving his car through it. Actor Arnold Schwarzenegger plays the **cyborg** known as the Terminator. He also speaks the same or a similar line in many later films.

Marlon Brando as Don Vito Corleone

Memorable Voices

It is not always the line that is remembered but the unique voice that delivers it. For example, Darth Vader of the Star Wars series has some memorable lines, but it is his deep voice and breathy speech that most people remember. Don Vito Corleone in *The Godfather* (1972) has a **muddled**, throaty voice that can be fun to imitate.

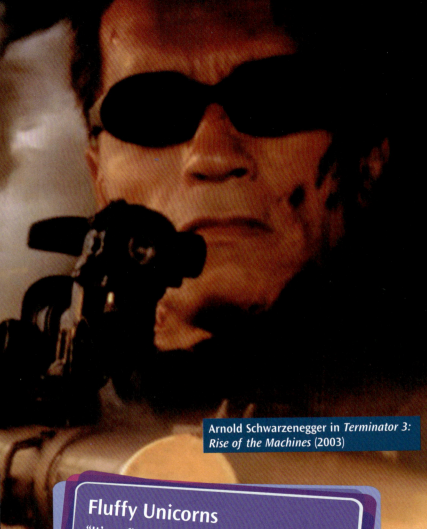

Arnold Schwarzenegger in *Terminator 3: Rise of the Machines* (2003)

Fluffy Unicorns

"It's so fluffy" became a popular line after the release of *Despicable Me* in 2010. As Agnes spots a stuffed unicorn, she cannot contain her excitement. Later, in *Despicable Me 3*, Agnes meets a man who has seen a real unicorn. She asks him, "Was it fluuuufffyyyy?"

Sean Connery as James Bond in
Diamonds Are Forever (1971)

Origin Story

When Fleming was writing the first Bond book, he saw a book called *Birds of the West Indies* by James Bond. Fleming loved the name so much that he called his character the same. He later told the real Bond's wife that they had "unlimited use of the name Ian Fleming for any purposes" and suggested they name "a particularly horrible species of bird" the *Ian Fleming*.

Go Ahead, Make My Day

Harry Calahan, a tough San Francisco detective, is the lead character in several Dirty Harry films. In 1983's *Sudden Impact*, Harry famously says to a criminal holding a gun, "Go ahead…make my day." After the movie was released, the line became an instant catchphrase.

Bond…James Bond

James Bond is a character created by Ian Fleming for a series of popular books. But the character is most famous for the ongoing movie series that feature this cool, larger-than-life spy. Bond's opening words in his first film, *Dr. No* (1962), are "Bond…James Bond." This iconic line (or a version of it) is spoken by Bond in several movies.

Men and Women

Many widely remembered lines come from male characters. It's often men who are featured in action films, which are usually made for young, male audiences by male filmmakers. Female characters in these films are few, and their combined spoken lines are far fewer than their male counterparts.

Nobody Puts Baby in a Corner!

In the popular film *Dirty Dancing* (1987), the star, "Baby," sits sadly in the corner until the hero, Johnny, struts in, reaches out, and pulls her up (both **literally** and **figuratively**). As he does so, Johnny declares, "Nobody puts Baby in a corner!" Audiences swoon over Johnny's swagger and boldness.

Patrick Swayze, as Johnny, dances with Baby, played by Jennifer Grey.

Truth, Justice, and the American Way

Superman first appeared in Action Comics in 1938. Since then, the "Man of Steel" has been featured in many comic books, movies, television shows, and more. His catchphrase is "truth, justice, and the American way." This phrase was heard in the *Adventures of Superman* radio program during World War II, when the United States was also fighting for those same things.

I Know

When Princess Leia tells Han Solo, "I love you," in *The Empire Strikes Back* (1980), the moment is heartbreaking. Solo is about to be frozen alive! Solo was supposed to answer Leia with "I love you, too," but Harrison Ford (who played Solo) and the director did not think this was right for his character. They changed Solo's response to "I know"—cementing it as one of the coolest lines in movie history.

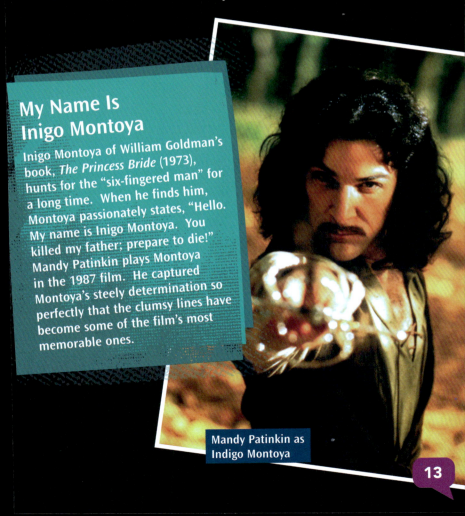

My Name Is Inigo Montoya

Inigo Montoya of William Goldman's book, *The Princess Bride* (1973), hunts for the "six-fingered man" for a long time. When he finds him, Montoya passionately states, "Hello. My name is Inigo Montoya. You killed my father; prepare to die!" Mandy Patinkin plays Montoya in the 1987 film. He captured Montoya's steely determination so perfectly that the clumsy lines have become some of the film's most memorable ones.

Mandy Patinkin as Indigo Montoya

I Solemnly Swear

When J. K. Rowling created the Marauder's Map for *Harry Potter and the Prisoner of Azkaban* (1999 book; 2004 film), she may have foreseen that the spells to open and close the map would become some of the most remembered lines from the Harry Potter series. The map is brought to life by declaring, "I solemnly swear that I am up to no good," and it is sealed with the phrase, "Mischief managed."

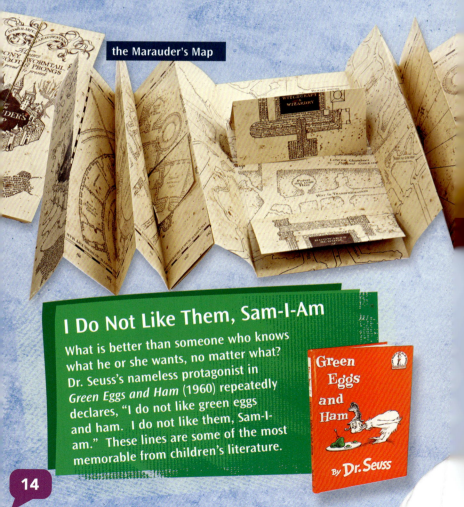

the Marauder's Map

I Do Not Like Them, Sam-I-Am

What is better than someone who knows what he or she wants, no matter what? Dr. Seuss's nameless protagonist in *Green Eggs and Ham* (1960) repeatedly declares, "I do not like green eggs and ham. I do not like them, Sam-I-am." These lines are some of the most memorable from children's literature.

Green Eggs and Ham
By Dr. Seuss

Show Me the Money!

When the movie *Jerry Maguire* (1996) premiered, it became a big hit with many memorable lines. One of the fan favorites is shouted by character Rod Tidwell (played by Cuba Gooding Jr.). Tidwell encourages the main character to "Show me the money!" and forces Jerry to shout the phrase passionately. Tidwell and his catchphrase come off as charming, funny, and very, very smooth.

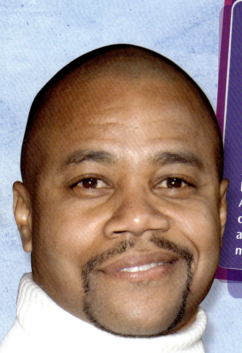

Cuba Gooding Jr.

Hello

Jerry Maguire is also known for another line, although this one is decidedly sweet. When Jerry rushes home to his wife to declare his love for her, she listens and then simply states, "You had me at 'hello.'" Audiences utter a collective "Awwww!" at this sweet and memorable line.

15

Powerful Phrases

Some lines are memorable because of the power behind them. The character who speaks the words might be a particularly powerful character. Or the words themselves might be inspiring or thrilling.

STOP! THINK...

Some images become just as memorable as the words or music they represent, particularly in film. You are probably familiar with this moment from the movie *The Lion King* (1994). Rafiki holds up the new prince (the cub, Simba), and the grassland animals all bow in respect.

- What makes a movie image iconic?
- How can a fictional scene become a representation of real, current events?
- Iconic images are commonly turned into memes. Why might that be so?

I Volunteer as Tribute

Katniss Everdeen is the protagonist of the Hunger Games book trilogy (2008–2010) by Suzanne Collins and the four movies (2012–2015) based on the series. The tone for the character is set early on when she takes her sister's place in the deadly Hunger Games. Realizing her sister could be killed in the tournament, Katniss refuses to remain silent. Fans likely didn't see it coming though when Katniss cries, "I volunteer as tribute!" Readers or audience members may gasp at the **magnitude** of her words.

Elizabeth Banks, as Effie Trinket, and Jennifer Lawrence, as Katniss Everdeen, in *The Hunger Games: Mockingjay—Part 2* (2015)

17

My Precious

Gollum of J. R. R. Tolkien's the Lord of the Rings book series (1954–1955) and *The Hobbit* (1937) is a key character across all of the story lines. He is even recreated in the accompanying movies (2001–2003; 2012–2014). Gollum may be best known for the haunting words he uses to describe the ring of power—"my precious." The scratchy voice that actor Andy Serkis gives Gollum may be as well-known as the words themselves.

I See Dead People

Writer and director M. Night Shyamalan first came to fame with his film *The Sixth Sense* (1999). In the movie, a young boy can see ghosts. He delivers the most famous line of the movie in a frightened whisper: "I see dead people."

No, I Am Your Father

Many people remember the line as "Luke, I am your father." But in the film *The Empire Strikes Back*, Darth Vader actually says, "No, I am your father." Either way, Luke is horrified at the **revelation**, and the entire Star Wars storyline changes course.

David Prowse as Darth Vader tells Mark Hamill's Luke Skywalker that he is Luke's father.

May the Force Be with You

Perhaps no line from the Star Wars series is more remembered and repeated than the signature phrase spoken by many characters across the movie **franchise**. It simply would not be Star Wars without "May the Force be with you." The line is offered as a type of blessing and protection and even inspired a Star Wars–themed day (May 4th).

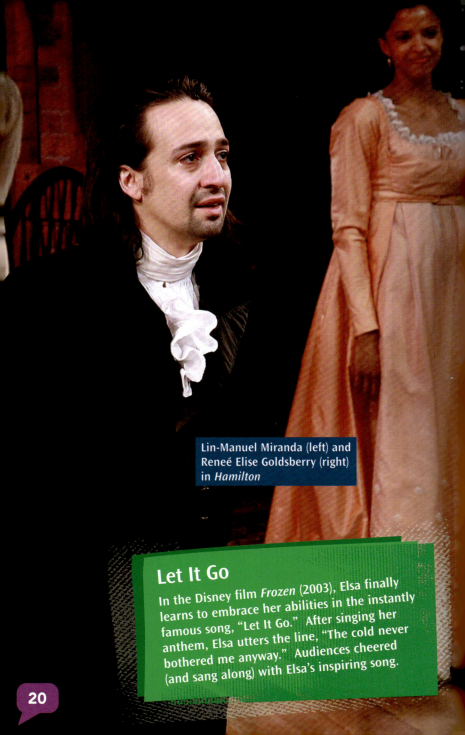

Lin-Manuel Miranda (left) and
Reneé Elise Goldsberry (right)
in *Hamilton*

Let It Go

In the Disney film *Frozen* (2003), Elsa finally learns to embrace her abilities in the instantly famous song, "Let It Go." After singing her anthem, Elsa utters the line, "The cold never bothered me anyway." Audiences cheered (and sang along) with Elsa's inspiring song.

My Shot

In 2015, the Broadway show *Hamilton*, written by and starring Lin-Manuel Miranda, took the world by storm. It tells the tale of Founding Father Alexander Hamilton and his **contemporaries**. The story flips **stereotypes** and expectations on their heads and is full of memorable lines. The most famous of all may be the one that repeatedly serves to define the **ambitious** lead character: "I am not throwing away my shot!"

It Was the Best of Times...

One of the most memorable opening lines of any work of literature is from Charles Dickens's *A Tale of Two Cities* (1859). The book opens with a long, conflicting description that captures the unrest of the time (the French Revolution). The line begins, "It was the best of times, it was the worst of times."

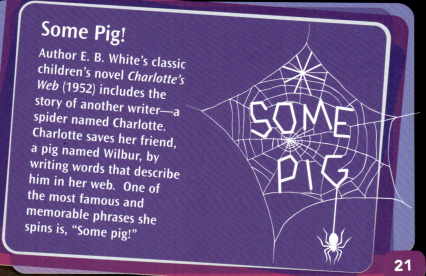

Some Pig!

Author E. B. White's classic children's novel *Charlotte's Web* (1952) includes the story of another writer—a spider named Charlotte. Charlotte saves her friend, a pig named Wilbur, by writing words that describe him in her web. One of the most famous and memorable phrases she spins is, "Some pig!"

From the Bard

William Shakespeare—commonly referred to as The Bard—is probably the most famous playwright in the world. He lived in England from 1564 to 1616. He is thought to have written at least 38 plays and 154 sonnets. What is most amazing, beyond the amount and mastery of his work, is the wealth of lines and phrases he wrote that have become part of everyday English. It is also surprising that most of his plays are regularly performed to this day. Here is a sampling of popular lines and phrases that originated with Shakespeare:

- All that glitters is not gold.
- be cruel only to be kind
- Be not afraid of greatness. Some are born great, some achieve greatness, and some have greatness thrust upon 'em.
- break the ice
- fair play
- forever and a day
- for goodness' sake
- full circle
- good riddance
- green-eyed monster

- I'll not budge an inch.
- Knock, knock! Who's there?
- lie low
- Love all, trust a few.
- Love is blind.
- off with his head
- one fell swoop
- Something wicked this way comes.
- The course of true love never did run smooth.
- The fault, dear Brutus, is not in our stars.
- too much of a good thing
- To thine own self be true.
- We have seen better days.
- wild goose chase

Miguel de Cervantes Saavedra

Most known for his classic work, *Don Quixote* (1605 and 1615), Cervantes is responsible for many phrases still used today. He wrote in Spanish, but like Shakespeare, his works have been translated into many other languages. Some famous Cervantes lines include: "a stone's throw," "cry my eyes out," "thank you for nothing," and "thou hast seen nothing yet." Interestingly, Shakespeare and Cervantes died within a day of each other!

To Be, or Not to Be

The title character of *Hamlet* (1603) is thinking about committing suicide when he speaks his famous line, "To be, or not to be: that is the question." The line begins a long **soliloquy** in which Hamlet considers death. Ultimately, he decides that, though his life may be bad, death would be worse.

Words from the Heart

As with many things in life, some lines stick with us because they are emotionally **charged**. We feel them, and so we remember them.

Here's Looking at You, Kid

Casablanca (1942) is considered by many critics to be one of the best movies of all time, filled with a wide range of memorable lines. One of those is, "Here's looking at you, kid," spoken by Rick (Humphrey Bogart) to Ilsa (Ingrid Bergman) as they leave one another forever. There is both charm and heartbreak in the line, which may be why it is remembered so well.

"We'll always have Paris," "Play it, Sam," and "Louis, I think this is the beginning of a beautiful friendship" are just a few of the many other memorable lines from the classic film.

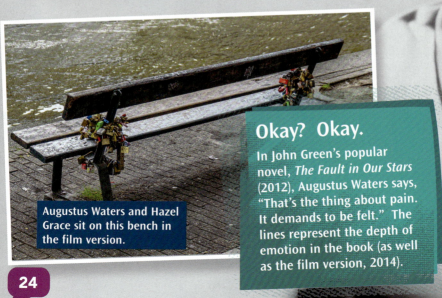

Augustus Waters and Hazel Grace sit on this bench in the film version.

Okay? Okay.

In John Green's popular novel, *The Fault in Our Stars* (2012), Augustus Waters says, "That's the thing about pain. It demands to be felt." The lines represent the depth of emotion in the book (as well as the film version, 2014).

A Contender

When Terry Malloy (played by Marlon Brando) of *On the Waterfront* (1954) cries out in misery, "I coulda been a contender," he is attacking his brother, Charley, for being a part of the problem that kept Terry from his dreams. It is a sad and bitter scene. The line is well remembered for the passion that Brando brought to its delivery.

Humphrey Bogart and Ingrid Bergman as Rick and Ilsa in *Casablanca*

25

No Place Like Home

In L. Frank Baum's book *The Wonderful Wizard of Oz* (1900), Dorothy tries to explain why she needs to leave Oz and go back home. She declares, "There is no place like home." In the movie *The Wizard of Oz* (1939), Dorothy uses the line "There's no place like home" as her means of actually going home. In both cases, the **sentiment** is sincere, and the line is well-remembered.

Judy Garland as Dorothy Gale in *The Wizard of Oz*

I'm Here

Celie of *The Color Purple* (1982) by Alice Walker is downtrodden. Her husband abuses her and tells her she is an ugly and worthless woman. Finally Celie stands up to him and leaves, memorably declaring that she may be poor, black, and ugly, "but I'm here."

E.T. Phone Home

E.T. the Extra-Terrestrial (1982) is the story of an adorable alien from another planet who ends up on Earth. The movie tugs at the audience's heartstrings as E.T. desperately seeks to find a way home. As he gathers the help he needs, he hurriedly learns a few words of English and tells his new friends what he wants—"E.T. home phone," to which the kids respond, "E.T. phone home!"

I'm the King of the World!

The film *Titanic* (1997) broke box office and awards records, but perhaps it is best remembered for an iconic line and image. As Jack Dawson (played by Leonardo DiCaprio) stands on the bow of the giant ship, arms outstretched, he cries out, "I'm the king of the world!" There is **bravado** in the line—but also humor, as perhaps best illustrated by the countless memes the image and line have inspired.

As You Wish

Viewers are given a final sweet moment at the end of *The Princess Bride*, when the grandfather responds to his grandson, "As you wish." Audiences know that he means, "I love you"—a reference to earlier scenes between the young couple of the film, Buttercup and Westley.

Cary Elwes's Westly holds hands with Robin Wright's Buttercup in *The Princess Bride*.

Hakuna Matata

The animated film *The Lion King* is set in Africa, where the characters Timon and Pumbaa attempt to enjoy a worry-free life. Their fun-loving life motto is the Swahili phrase *hakuna matata*. A rough translation of the phrase is "no worries."

Stay Gold, Ponyboy, Stay Gold

S. E. Hinton was in high school when she wrote *The Outsiders* (1967), which became a hit film in 1983. Johnny has been badly injured and is near death when he offers the best life advice to his young friend, Ponyboy: "Stay gold, Ponyboy, stay gold." Johnny is referring to a Robert Frost poem that Ponyboy had read aloud when the two were on the run. Johnny is advising Ponyboy to hold on to his innocence.

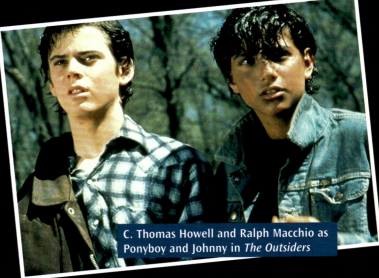

C. Thomas Howell and Ralph Macchio as Ponyboy and Johnny in *The Outsiders*

Always

Severus Snape in the Harry Potter series (1997–2007) does not like Harry. But he loves Harry's mother, Lily, who was killed when Harry was a baby. Albus Dumbledore is surprised to learn that Snape's love for Lily motivates his protection of Harry. This truth is revealed in the memorable exchange between Dumbledore and Snape:

"After all this time?

"Always."

It Was Beauty Killed the Beast

One of the most memorable lines in movie history is repeated in each major remake of the film, *King Kong* (1933, 1976, 2005). The giant ape falls to his death while trying to defend himself against a swarm of airplanes. But Kong is also protecting Ann Darrow, an actress widely considered beautiful. In response to the scene, Darrow's director, Carl Denham, **poignantly** declares, "It was Beauty killed the Beast."

Rosebud

Citizen Kane (1941) is praised by many as the best film ever made. It is the story of a rich newspaper owner, Charles Foster Kane (played by Orson Welles, who also directed, produced, and co-wrote the film). Kane's dying word is "Rosebud," and a reporter is determined to find out what it means. In the end, the audience finds out that "Rosebud" was the name of Kane's childhood sled. The line is a key to understanding Kane's character.

One Can See Rightly

The Little Prince (1943) is a classic French novel by Antoine de Saint-Exupéry (ahn-TWAN duh san-teg-zoo-pey-REE). It tells the story of a pilot who is stranded in a desert. The pilot meets a prince who has come to Earth from another planet. The story is fantastical and moving. One of the most famous lines from the book and its adaptation is, "It is only with the heart that one can see **rightly**."

Change Your Stars

In the film *A Knight's Tale* (2001), John Thatcher sends away his young son, William, as an apprentice in an attempt to give the boy a better life. Thatcher tells his son, "Change your stars, and live a better life than I have." The notion of "changing your stars" is repeated throughout the film until William returns home to show his father he has done just that.

King Kong holds Ann Darrow (played by Naomi Watts) at the end of the 2005 version of *King Kong*.

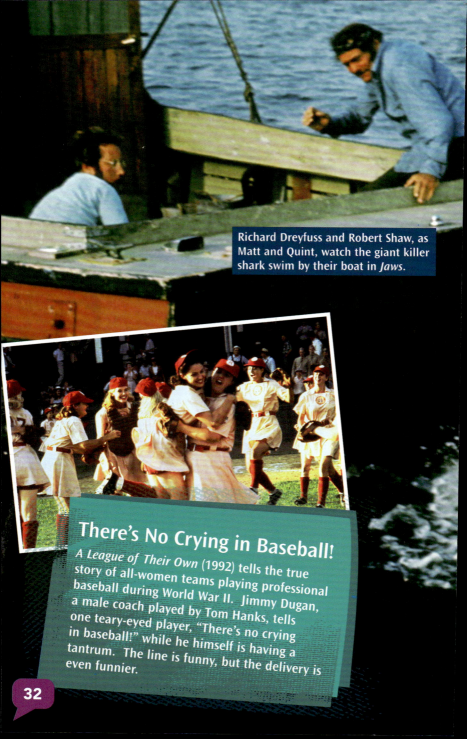

Richard Dreyfuss and Robert Shaw, as Matt and Quint, watch the giant killer shark swim by their boat in *Jaws*.

There's No Crying in Baseball!

A League of Their Own (1992) tells the true story of all-women teams playing professional baseball during World War II. Jimmy Dugan, a male coach played by Tom Hanks, tells one teary-eyed player, "There's no crying in baseball!" while he himself is having a tantrum. The line is funny, but the delivery is even funnier.

Funny Lines

Funny lines tend to stick with us. If it makes us laugh, we want to remember it and laugh all over again. The funny line may be witty, silly, or bitingly ironic—but it always seems worth repeating.

You're Gonna Need a Bigger Boat

Jaws (1975) is not a funny movie. It is the suspenseful story of a 25-foot killer shark that terrorizes a beachfront community. The movie is known for its **menacing** music (daaaaa-dum, daaaaa-dum) that plays when the shark is coming, but it is also known for actor Roy Scheider's **ad-libbed** line when his character first spots the shark off the side of a fishing boat: "You're gonna need a bigger boat."

Hello, Gorgeous!

Barbra Streisand stars in *Funny Girl* (1968) as Fanny Brice, who rises to fame on Broadway in the early twentieth century. Fanny's story is both inspiring and heartbreaking, but Fanny herself is very funny. Her classic line is one she delivers while looking at her newly glamorous self in a mirror: "Hello, gorgeous!"

Life Was Like a Box of Chocolates

Forrest Gump (1994) is a movie that is bursting with iconic images and sayings, but it also creates its own. Forrest speaks one of his most well-remembered lines as he waits for a bus while holding a box of candy. Forrest tells a stranger who is also waiting, "My mama always said life was like a box of chocolates...you never know what you're gonna get." The line is both funny and sweet.

Barbra Streisand as Fanny Brice in *Funny Girl*

Here's Johnny!

The Shining was a novel by Stephen King (1977) and then a hit movie (1980), but it is the movie that features one of its most iconic lines. The line serves as **comic relief** but is also terrifying. As crazed hotel keeper Jack Torrance chases his wife with an ax, he breaks a hole in the door, peeks inside, and calls, "Heeeere's Johnny"—mimicking the famous tagline of a late-night television host.

Tom Hanks in *Forrest Gump*

Fronkenshteen

Young Frankenstein (1974) was directed and co-written by Mel Brooks, who also created the hit musical play (2007). It is the story of Dr. Frederick Frankenstein, who tries to distance himself from his famous ancestor, Victor. But just the same, he winds up working to bring the dead back to life. Both the movie and play are very funny and filled with memorable lines. "It's pronounced 'Fronkenshteen,'" is just one of many of them.

As Dead as a Door-nail

A Christmas Carol (1843) is one of the most famous adapted ghost stories. Its plot is classic and the characters iconic. The Charles Dickens novel ends the first paragraph with a famous line: "Old Marley was as dead as a door-nail."

Gene Wilder, as Dr. Frankenstein, celebrates his success in bringing a dead man (played by Peter Boyle) back to life.

We're Not in Kansas Anymore

The Wizard of Oz begins with Dorothy and her dog, Toto, riding a tornado from Kansas to Oz. In the film, Dorothy looks around at the strange new world and says, "Toto, I've got a feeling we're not in Kansas anymore." The **understatement** of the line made it instantly memorable.

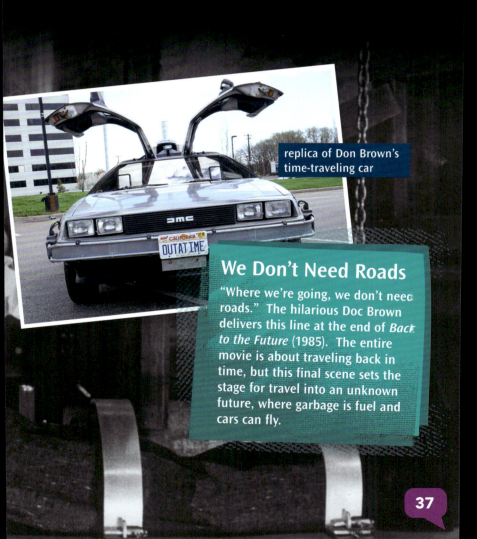

replica of Don Brown's time-traveling car

We Don't Need Roads

"Where we're going, we don't need roads." The hilarious Doc Brown delivers this line at the end of *Back to the Future* (1985). The entire movie is about traveling back in time, but this final scene sets the stage for travel into an unknown future, where garbage is fuel and cars can fly.

Don't Call Me Shirley

The **deadpan**, literal comedy in the movie *Airplane!* (1980) is extremely quotable, and dedicated fans can **recite** nearly the entire movie by heart. A favorite joke sequence of many viewers is presented for the first time in this way:

"Surely you can't be serious."
"I am serious, and don't call me Shirley."

Take the Cannoli

While the story of *The Godfather* (1969 book; 1972 film) is dramatic and sad, there are also funny moments—usually ironically so. One of the most remembered lines comes after Rocco shoots Paulie, who has betrayed the family. As Rocco and mobster Clemenza attempt to cover their tracks, Clemenza tells Rocco, "Leave the gun. Take the cannoli."

Let the Wild Rumpus Start!

Maurice Sendak's imaginative, hilarious, and touching book *Where the Wild Things Are* (1963 book; 2009 film) is a classic childhood favorite for many people. One delightful line is particularly memorable and often repeated. As soon as Max, the protagonist, is crowned king of the wild things, he proclaims, "Let the wild **rumpus** start!" Children everywhere are delighted to **comply**.

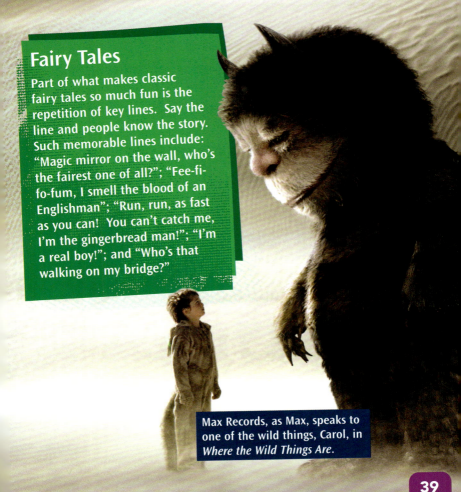

Fairy Tales

Part of what makes classic fairy tales so much fun is the repetition of key lines. Say the line and people know the story. Such memorable lines include: "Magic mirror on the wall, who's the fairest one of all?"; "Fee-fi-fo-fum, I smell the blood of an Englishman"; "Run, run, as fast as you can! You can't catch me, I'm the gingerbread man!"; "I'm a real boy!"; and "Who's that walking on my bridge?"

Max Records, as Max, speaks to one of the wild things, Carol, in *Where the Wild Things Are.*

I've Got a Million of 'Em

Actor and comedian Jimmy Durante (1893–1980) often followed his **corniest** jokes with a winking smile and the line, "I've got a million of 'em." In fact, people still quote Durante (whether knowingly or not) after they have said or done something funny.

Durante's classic line can be used in reference to memorable quotations, too. There are a million of 'em! We remember favorite lines from movies, literature, plays, advertising, television, music, and more. They can come from anywhere and instantly become part of popular culture and common language.

So, "Hasta la vista, baby." "Have fun storming the castle," and "may the odds be ever in your favor!"

You can quote me on that.

Jimmy Durante

Wrong!

One thing about memorable lines is that many people often misquote them! For example, Neil Armstrong's famous line as he walked on the moon is not, "That's one small step for man, one giant leap for mankind." Armstrong actually said, "That's one small step for *a* man…." One little word can make all the difference!

Neil Armstrong

What's That From?

Some lines are so memorable, you may know them without even knowing where they come from. Here are a few favorites and their origins: "Hasta la vista, baby" is said in *Terminator 2: Judgment Day* (1991) before the main character shoots the villain. "Have fun storming the castle!" is from *The Princess Bride*, as Miracle Max and Valerie wish the heroes good luck. "May the odds be ever in your favor" is the catchphrase of Effie Trinket from The Hunger Games (books and movies).

Glossary

ad-libbed—made up on the spot instead of planned

ambitious—having a desire to be powerful, successful, or famous

bravado—brave or confident talk or behavior that is intended to impress other people

catchphrases—words or phrases that are commonly used to represent a person or group

charged—causing or showing strong emotions

comic relief—funny line or moment that provides a break from tension, stress, or other drama

comply—to do or go along with what someone has been asked to do

contemporaries—people from the same time period

corniest—silly or old-fashioned

cyborg—a person whose body contains electrical or mechanical devices, which give him or her abilities that are greater than those of normal humans

deadpan—describes humor that is said or done in a serious way without showing emotions

figuratively—having a meaning different from the stated meaning and expressing an idea that describes something else

franchise—a series that shares the same settings, characters, or other unifying events

ironic—finding something funny or strange because it is different from what you expected

lexicon—words used by a person or group of people

literally—meaning exactly as stated

lore—the traditional beliefs, stories, and knowledge that relate to a certain subject, place, or group of people

magnitude—size or importance of something

menacing—referring to a dangerous or possibly harmful thing or person

muddled—unclear or confusing

plethora—a large amount

poignantly—causing a strong feeling of sadness

recite—to read or say something out loud from memory

revelation—act of revealing a secret fact in a surprising way

rightly—correctly

rumpus—a noisy commotion or disturbance

sentiment—an opinion or attitude

signature—closely associated with someone or something

soliloquy—a long speech that a character in a play makes to an audience, which reveals his or her inner thoughts

stereotypes—often unfair and untrue beliefs that many people have about people of certain groups

understatement—a statement that makes something seem less important or smaller than it really is

Index

Check It Out!

Books

Bartlett, John. 2012. *Bartlett's Familiar Quotations, 18th edition*. New York: Little, Brown and Company.

Demakis, Joseph M. 2012. *The Ultimate Book of Quotations*. Charleston: CreateSpace.

Fullmer, Brogan L. 2010. *Quotes of Note: Brilliant Thoughts Arranged by Subject*. Charleston: CreateSpace

Shakespeare, William. 2012. *Shakespeare: A Book of Quotations*. Mineola: Dover Publications.

Websites

American Film Institute. *AFI's 100 Greatest Movie Quotes of All Time*. www.afi.com/100years/quotes.aspx.

Goodreads. *Popular Quotes*. www.goodreads.com/quotes.

IMDB. IMDB Chart's Top Rated Movies. www.imdb.com/chart/top.

Try It!

It is common practice for people to rattle off quotes they know from favorite movies, books, and more. But what if you could speak only in quotations?

Write a short script with at least two characters discussing a problem they are having. For the dialogue, use only quotations from other published sources. Sources include:

- advertisements
- books
- movies
- plays
- songs
- television shows

About the Author

Dona Herweck Rice has written hundreds of books, stories, and essays for kids of all ages on topics of all kinds, from animals to zombies and everything in between. Writing is her superpower, although she has yet to find the right cape to go with her reading glasses and ink-stained fingertips. She also loves reading, live theater, dancing anytime and anywhere, and a good hammock on a summer afternoon. Rice was a teacher and is an acting coach, director, and blogger. She lives in California with her husband, two sons, and a cute but neurotic little dog.